"I'm Single...A

by Cynthia Mitchell, Aiken, South Carolina. All rights reserved. Printed in the United States of America. No part of this publication may be reproduced, stored in a retrieval system or transmitted in any form or by any means without prior permission of the Author except in the case of brief quotations embodied in critical articles and reviews. For more information, contact Cynthia Mitchell at joyfullpublishing@gmail.com.

Scripture taken from the HOLY BIBLE, NEW INTERNATIONAL VERSION ® Copyright © 1973, 1978, 1984 by International Bible Society. Used by permission of Zondervan Publishing House. All rights reserved. The "NIV" and "New International Version" trademarks are registered in the United States Patent and Trademark Office by International Bible Society. Use of either trademark requires the permission of International Bible Society.

ISBN 978-0-9789044-4-9

Table of Contents

Acknowledgements

The Prelude   **page 5**
    In My Season of Singleness

The Plan of Marriage   **page 11**
    Abigail or Jezebel

The Pain of Divorce   **page 19**
    He Loves Me. He Loves Me Not

The Process of Healing   **page 25**
    Assume the Position

The Problem with Waiting   **page 29**
    "Lady In Waiting"

The Promise of the Father   **page 35**
    I Will Never Leave You

The Provision for Living   **page 41**
    "...our Daily Bread..."

The Postlude   **page 47**
    Timing Is Everything

The Prologue   **page 53**
    #myturningpoint

The Prelude
YOU are before before. YOU are after after.
Cynthia Mitchell

In My Season of Singleness
To everything there is a season, and a time to every purpose under the heaven.
Ecclesiastes 3:1

"To everything there is a season..." Boy, that is sooooo easy to say. It just rolls off your tongue like butter. It is much more difficult to digest and discern. Why can't we plant corn this morning and have it for dinner tonight?

According to Ecclesiastes 3:1, there is a TIME for every (mine and yours) purpose under the heaven. Are you under the heaven? *Since you're reading this, please say yes.* There is an appointed time for your purpose. There may be nothing in this writing that you have not heard before – probably a million times over. But come, let us reason together and examine some nagging thoughts and questions.

For the purpose of this writing, I have identified five foundational facts on which to establish our reasoning process.
 1) Hebrews 11:6 - But without faith it is impossible to please Him. For he that cometh to God must believe that He is and that He is a rewarder of them that diligently seek Him.

We must first determine if we are believers in and of Christ. Believing in God is one thing while believing what He says is something totally else. Knowing that your name is Sally Sue has nothing to do with whether or not you can be trusted to pick me up for work on time like you said you would. We must have faith that God will perform His Word as He has spoken. If, and only if, we are able to simply take God at His Word can we proceed to the next foundational fact.

> *2) 2 Timothy 3:16 - All scripture is given by inspiration of God and is profitable for doctrine, for reproof, for correction, for instruction in righteousness.*

God's Word is productive in every area of our lives. Be encouraged and know that God has spoken some awesome words over us. Words that are good for doctrine – foundation on which to base decisions and establish a lifestyle pleasing to Him. Words for chastisement and correction so that we don't run the risk of straying too far from his ark of safety. We must, however, be diligent in receiving what He's said.

3) 1Peter 5:7- Casting all your care on Him, for He careth for you.
God is concerned about EVERY aspect of our lives. *This would be a good time to count your many blessings. See what the Lawd has done.* Think about the little things that we take for granted, but with deeper thought, realize how thoroughly concerned God is about even the smallest detail of our lives. We just expect to get up and breathe every morning. We don't sit and think – okay breathe in. Breathe out. But when the truth is told, you realize that if God didn't give you your next breath, you couldn't catch it, not even in a fast car. God intimately cares for you and me.

4) 2 Peter 3:8- But beloved, be not ignorant of this one thing, that one day is with the Lord as a thousand years, and a thousand years as one day.

Hmmm. God's timing and our timing are not the same. God is not confined by time. Psalm 90:2 explains that He was God before the mountains, earth and world were formed - - from everlasting to everlasting. *He was **before** before and will be **after** after.*

So given these four foundational facts, we can know

that God sees our tears, hears our cries, He is able to meet our every need and will do so in His time.

For the most part, we know that. It's just that often times in our season of singleness, we get sidetracked...impatient...confused. We begin to allow too many outside influences to affect our thinking and ultimately our actions. Hopefully, what is shared in this writing will help you avoid some of the many pitfalls that are found during your season of singleness. *You gotta experience some of the pitfalls, that's what makes the journey interesting enough to get up everyday.*

Hold on. We did say that we would establish five foundational facts. Didn't we?

> *5) Psalm 139:14- I will praise thee for I am fearfully and wonderfully made. Marvelous are thy works and that my soul knoweth right well.*

God has made each and every one of us a marvelous, individual workmanship of His own hands. We are not a carbon copy of any other human being nor did we come hot off the press of a cookie cutter factory. There is absolutely nothing wrong with being single. We have been conditioned to believe that being single is a bad thing. An attempt to elaborate on the subject of "singleness" is not necessary. Dr. Myles Munroe does and excellent job in his book "Single, Married, Separated and Life After Divorce." Any attempt to add to that would be feeble, to say the least. In a nutshell, God made us single, separate and individual beings and like it or not, we are all going to stay that way. Establish your identity in Christ. Period. No matter who comes or who goes.

I do not claim any authority on relationship matters or the institution of marriage. Frankly, I may be THE LAST person you want to advise you on the subject. I just want to share my truth about the Plan, the Pain, the Process, the Problem, the Promise and the Provision as related to marriage, divorce, healing and waiting. Shall we?

The Plan of Marriage

If we are incapable of finding peace in ourselves, it is pointless to search elsewhere.
Francois de la Rochefoucauld

Abigail or Jezebel

"Dearly beloved, we are gathered here today in the sight of God to witness..." That's scary. When two people stand together entering the holy bonds of matrimony, God is watching. He is a witness. Does He flip the channel if the two standing are not the right two? Does God turn away if the bride and groom have not followed His prescribed plan for marriage? What is He saying? What is He thinking? Is God pleased? Is this union a part of His plan?

Then the Lord God said, "It is not good that the man should be alone; I will make him a helper fit for him." Genesis 2:18

The Plan of Marriage includes complete singleness before and during marriage.

The object of the game for a Christian couple is for two single, separate individuals to compliment, enhance, support, encourage and assist each other in the fulfillment of individual and collective destiny. Our personalities, ministry styles, skills and abilities should complement each other. A mate does not complete me. Christ did that. Too many of us are looking for someone to complete us. *Wrong answer.*

Separate and complete. This concept is often difficult to grasp even when you've been married and divorced. Maybe I should say ESPECIALLY if you've married and divorced. According to Genesis 2:18, the man was made THEN the "helper fit for him" was made. Two single and separate beings. We have believed so many lies about ourselves individually and collectively. It's time to examine ourselves in the Light of God's Word.

So God created man in His own image, in the image of God He created Him; male and female He created them. And God blessed them, and God said to them, "Be fruitful and multiply, and fill the earth and subdue it; and have dominion over the fish of the sea and over the birds of the air and over every living thing that moves upon the earth."
Genesis 1:27-28

The Plan of Marriage is for procreation and for the two to manage the earth's resources together.

But because of the temptation to immorality, each man should have his own wife and each woman her own husband. The husband should give to his wife her conjugal rights, and likewise the wife to her husband. 1 Corinthians 7:2-3

The Plan of Marriage is to avoid fornication.

Sexual intercourse is the most intimate physical act between two people. When you open yourself up to that level of sharing with someone, you also open yourself to spirits that are attached to your partner. If you've never heard Dr. Juanita Bynum's "No More Sheets", you need to get the video. Let it bless and set you free. When we "hook up" with someone, we exchange habits and characteristics. I get a little of you and you get a little of me. When we continue to make that sort of exchange with multiple partners the result can be catastrophic. For women it means that we receive too many "personalities" into our womb/"birthing place". And it causes a man's strength to be diluted and his seed scattered. A part of the plan of marriage is to avoid this trap of the enemy. A husband and wife are to cover each other completely under the covenant of marriage.

Wherefore they are no more twain but one flesh. What therefore God hath joined together, let not man put asunder. Matthew 19:6

The Plan of Marriage is intended to be permanent.

I'm certain we've all heard the wedding ring analogy. You know, how the wedding band is a perfect circle - no beginning, no end.

In MY perfect world, a shonuff Kingdom king (my husband) and his Kingdom queen (me) should be building life, ministry and businesses - - - together. *Runnin' thangs!* Together we exercise authority over resources in the earth. Where his ruling skills and abilities stop, mine start and vice versa. We work like a hand in glove, a finely tuned machine in sync with the moving of the Holy Spirit and each other. Not only that, we are to reproduce ourselves in our children and teach them, by example, how to do the same. Their ministries, businesses and accomplishments should surpass ours. That's in my perfect world. However, in **this** world - - *well check out the title of the book you're reading.* ☺

Proverbs 18:22 says, "he who finds a wife finds a good thing and obtains favor from the Lord." (**Disclaimer: This part is for women only**. *Men leave the room.*) Do men really want a wife? See, 'cause I've talked to some brothers who **say** they want a wife but the more you talk with them about their vision of a mate, it seems that what they really want is one of three things:

(1) A poodle – no thinking required. She doesn't have to do or be anything other than be pretty. *Cool. I ain't hatin'.*

(2) Another mother – limited thinking required. In this case, a woman's most valuable asset is her domestic skills. *Let me tell you like my grandma used to say: "dis ain't no slavey time."*

(3) A legal sex partner – again, no thinking required or domestic skills for that matter.

*Shhh. Don't tell the men but a **real** wife is a mixture of the three and then some.*

The way I see it ladies, we are all working with the same equipment. It's all about how we use it.

Okay men, you can come back now.

So, let's look at two women. Abigail and Jezebel. *Same equipment* However, there are stark differences between the two. According to 1 Samuel 25, Abigail was originally married to a "mean and surly" man by the name of Nabal. Even though she was married to a fool, Abigail showed herself to be discerning, discreet and direct in a way that did not disrespect herself or her husband. Jezebel, wife of wicked king Ahab, (1 Kings 16) on the other hand, was disruptive, deceitful and destructive to the point of her own demise. Both women were married to men with less than desirable qualities. *Same "make"* While one used her attributes and femininity to bring about peace, the other used hers to create chaos. *Different "models"*.

There is so much to be said regarding the genetic makeup of women; the intricacies, essence and creating powers of wo-man. I cannot even begin to adequately explain or address all that I have come to understand about who I am as Woman. I do know this. We cheapen the sacred assignment for which we were created when we wield sex/sexuality as a weapon or prize.

The Pain of Divorce
"One man's junk is another man's joy!"
Cynthia Mitchell

He Loves Me. He Loves Me Not.

And Pharisees came up to Him and tested Him by asking, "is it lawful to divorce one's wife for any cause?" He answered, "have you not read that he who made them from the beginning made them male and female, and said, 'for this reason a man shall leave his father and mother and be joined to his wife, and the two shall become one flesh'? So they are no longer two but one flesh. What therefore God has joined together, let no man put asunder." They said to him, "why then did Moses command one to give a certificate of divorce, and to put her away?' He said to them, "for your hardness of heart Moses allowed you to divorce your wives, but from the beginning it was not so." Matthew 19:3-8

The Pain of Divorce was not a part of God's original plan and starts with hardness of heart.

I can't tell you how many seasoned "Christian" couples I have observed who really seem to not even like each other. They function effectively in their respective ministry roles, live in nice homes, wear beautiful clothes and drive immaculate automobiles but their personal interaction could be described as terse, at the least. I don't know when or where their "hardness" began. I do have an idea of how. Often rejection, abuse, circumstances and situations set in motion before we were even born contribute greatly to our hardness of heart. I don't have an easy 3 or 12 step plan to deal with hardness of heart issues. It may just be a good time to do a personal assessment and get rid of all the junk that has accumulated. This is NOT the time to recount everything your spouse/ex said and did wrong. *Which, I'm sure is plenty.* ☺ Remind yourself, "I can't deal with another person's heart issues neither can anyone else deal with mine". *In this case, it really is "every man for himself".*

The Pain of Divorce causes a ripple effect.

Divorce often opens the door to devastation in other areas such as economics, spiritual walk, mental, emotional and physical health. Let me try to describe what the pain of divorce felt like for me. Imagine having both arms ripped from your body. I mean just torn right out of the socket. You're left with two huge, gaping wounds - - muscle, ligaments and bone exposed. There's blood gushing everywhere. You can't do anything to stop the excruciating pain or the bleeding. After a while some well-meaning church or family member walks up and gives you one band aid.

I realize that my coping strategy was "stay busy". It was not a conscious plan. Survival mode just kicked in and it became hard to turn off. Work, church events, the children's activities were stacked on top of each other for many years. I would like to think that my initial "busy time" was a good thing. It did allow some time for the hurt and anger to burn itself off before I had to really deal with it. On the other hand, I don't know that it helped me as far as taking time and energy to build and sustain a real relationship. As I reflect on that time in my life, I know that some of the "sorry" men I encountered had a lot of room to remain "sorry" simply because I was so busy "making it happen" that I didn't always call them out on their "sorryness". At the same time, it is quite possible that I let a couple of good ones get away because of my lack of attention to them. *Sigh* Please identify and utilize good coping strategies for your situation. Don't let it become a crutch and stay there too long.

I did not get married to divorce. *Does anybody?* Having experienced divorce, I can honestly say that I will never be the same. There is no going back to the days, weeks and months prior to July 19, 1986 when I was a footloose and fancy free military woman. The whole world ahead of me. *No turning back. No turning back.*

If you are not completely single prior to marriage, then experience divorce, it only adds to your root problems. It's like you already didn't have a clear indication of who you are but the one thing you now know is that you are a failure. At least, that's what you think. So, the unclear picture is now further distorted. The enemy's got you right where he wants you – confused. BUT what if God has a plan in and for the pain?

Yes, the pain of divorce has forever changed me. I am not the same as before. I am more resourceful and resilient than I ever knew. I will never, EVER be the same again. I am stronger. I am better.

The Process of Healing

Circumstances are the rulers of the weak; but they are the instruments of the wise.

Samuel Lover

Assume the Position

To the choirmaster. A Psalm of David. I waited patiently for the Lord; He inclined to me and heard my cry. Psalm 40:1

The Process of Healing requires patience in the presence of God.

"...He inclined unto me and heard my cry." The process of healing includes a wide range of emotions - - anger, sadness, relief, fear. Sometimes we can do ourselves a disservice by tying to move on too fast. We seek to numb the pain with activity. Go on - scream, kick and cry. After all, how can God incline to you if He can't hear your cry? You don't have to be strong all the time. God's strength is made perfect in our weakness (2 Corinthians 12:9).

In my trying to move on too fast, I became over extended in credit (there was always more month than money) and other responsibilities. I was in a hurry to establish some sort of normalcy for the children. *What is normal?*

I remember that I stopped praying for more resources and asked God to show me how to be a good steward of what I already had. I had to learn how to stop wanting so much so fast and allow the process of time to develop patience in me. (James 1:2-4). I had to learn the way to the presence of God.

Enter into His gates with thanksgiving, and into His courts with praise: be thankful unto Him, and bless His name. Psalm 100:4

We think "entering into His gates" means going to church but our ultimate desired location is not a building it is the very presence of God. We begin the journey into His presence with thanksgiving and continue with sincere praise until our will is broken and we submit in worship through our lifestyle. Getting involved with Church activities is not the answer. It's a smoke screen. We often talk about the tools of the enemy and this may be one of the biggest. Being involved with auxiliaries, committees and functions is not the roadmap into God's presence.

Positions of Patience
    Position # 1 – up lifted hands in Thanksgiving

    Position #2 – an open mouth in praise

Position #3 – a bowed spirit in worship

There have been so many times when I didn't have a dime to my name or a friend to call my own but I would practice getting into the presence of God. That's all I had. Little did I know, it's all I really needed. This is not an attempt to get super spiritual on you. Simply praying, praising and worshipping will not pay the bills and does bring the physical companionship that we desire. It does, however, help us reach the heart of the Father, who then releases to us strategy for how to live, become better stewards of the resources we have and how to get what we don't have. Prayer, Praise and Worship bring revelation regarding how we should position ourselves in anticipation while we wait..........

The Problem With Waiting
I want it all. I want it now.
Cynthia Mitchell

Lady In Waiting

If Job waited on the Lord, tell me why can't I? Could it be that I have not been convinced that what lies ahead of me is better and far greater than what's behind me? Could it be that I have been conditioned by society's microwave mentality? Gotta go. Gotta go...now. Gotta have it. Gotta have it...now. Everything, everybody is in a hurry. Always gotta go somewhere. Always gotta be somewhere.

After the release of my first book, I participated in a Writers' Workshop. My staff (my children) were on duty as usual, setting up, organizing and helping out with odds and ends. During the session, which was quite lengthy, my staff sat "patiently" at the back of the room. I thought my son, in particular, was being quite observant and taking in some of the talks. Several months later I found his notes from the day in his room. I would like to share an excerpt with you.

12:43 -I sit and I am bored.
12:44 -I still sit and I am still bored.
12:45 -Still sitting. Still bored.
12:46 -Yep. Bored and sitting.
12:47 -Help me!
12:48 -????????????????????

12:49 -!!!!!!!!!!!!!!!!!!!!!!!!!!!!!
12:50 -ZZZZZZZZZZZZZZZ
12:51 -I awaken.
12:52 -Bored and sitting.
12:53 -I stand up!
12:54 -I breathe.
12:55 -Got some water.
12:56 -Kick a chair.
12:57 -Wish I hadn't.
12:58 -Bored.
12:59 -More bored.
1:00 -Will this torture ever end?!

Will this torture ever end? That's a good question.

I find it interesting that so much of what we do in the spirit is likened to what we, as women, must do in the process of giving birth. We are impregnated – someone speaks a Word into our spirit and it begins to grow. At first the growth is barely noticeable. Changes are small. A missed period, which is usually a regular occurrence, gets our attention. *Hmm. "The things I used to do, I don't do no more."* Then clothes begin to get a little tight. You notice that you don't fit into old situations and places anymore – you know, like in the presence of gossip and foul language. *"The places I used to go, I don't go no more."* Basically, there is not a lot to do during the pregnancy. You simply continue to eat properly (study the Word so that it gets IN you.) Make proper adjustments to accommodate your growth (spend time in prayer and fellowship with like believers) and just wait out the gestation period. You wait until the life in you is ready to come out.

You wait - - patiently.

Two particular women in Scripture had to wait through some unflattering circumstances. Mary (Luke 1:27-35), an unmarried girl, received a ridiculous Word from God that she was about to birth The Messiah. Rahab (Joshua 2:1-14), a "seasoned business woman" took hold of a promise from two strange men then had to wait, amid questioning and scrutiny, for that promise to materialize. 1. Being "blessed and highly favored" will often come with its share of discomfort. 2. It may be necessary to endure whispers and stares while you wait for the "promise". 3. Some things folk say about you during your waiting season will be true. *This was not the FIRST time strange men went into Rahab's house during the night.* So what? Get it together. Do better. Move on.

For the record, patience has never been my strong suit. One of my favorite poems is by Ruth Harms Calkin.

"I know I need more patience, Lord. But I simply cannot create it. I plead with you to do it for me. And Lord, could you hurry a little?"

I've taken notice of Jesus' experience with waiting in Psalm 40:1. According to the "Thru the Bible" commentary by J. Vernon McGhee, "Psalm 40 is a messianic Psalm. It reveals that the death of Christ was not a defeat, at all. It was, in fact, a great victory. When He (referring to Christ) says 'I waited patiently for the Lord and He inclined unto me and heard my cry', He is referring to His cry from the cross."

Imagine that. Jesus cried while waiting during His "cross" experience. On the way to fulfilling His ultimate purpose of conquering death, hell and the grave, it was absolutely necessary that Jesus endure the agony of WAITING on the cross.

Jesus showed up knowing Who, Whose and Why He was sent. He embraced the cross experience because He knew what to expect at the end. Could it be that we are going through one cross experience after the other *"waitin' on the Lawd"* but we're not really even sure why? The old saints told us God's gonna work it out. But if I don't know what I'm waiting for, how do I know when it's worked out?

I've told the story many times of being in the room with my cousin when she gave birth to her first child. Three of us walked into the birthing room. My pregnant cousin, her husband with his lunch sack, and me, with my purse. As time, and her pain, progressed, the excitement and anticipation grew. Every time the doctor gave the instruction to push, we all pushed. We all went in <u>wanting</u> a baby and participated in the process in some way. But when it was all said and done, her husband left the room with his lunch sack and I left with my purse. The only one who left that birthing room with a baby is the only one who went into the room actively <u>expecting</u> a baby.

Jeremiah 29:11
For I know the thoughts that I think toward you, saith the Lord. Thoughts of peace and not of evil, to give you an expected end.

What does God expect of and for you? What do you expect of God and for yourself?

The Promise of The Father
All I have seen teaches me to trust the Creator for all I have not seen.
Ralph Waldo Emerson

I Will Never Leave You

"On my honor, I will try to do my duty to serve God and my country, to help other people at all times and to obey the Girl Scout law". Mrs Mamie Lundy's Girl Scout Troop #30 taught us a thing or two about promises and "keepin ya word". What happens though, when two people make a promise and one doesn't keep their part of it?

If we are doing this thing called "life" properly then we should continuously grow and evolve. The person you kiss at the altar will develop over the years. There should be signs of maturing as the relationship progresses. I don't know that anyone will, can or should grow out of their basic identity, though. Okay, so THAT takes me all the way back to the first chapter of my previous book (Oh, Joy! ©2006 Joy!Full Publishing) where I asked the question: Just who do you think you are? Maybe the question SHOULD be, "Who are you? Really." That applies to both parties. Did you stand there and promise "I do" knowing all along that you don't, can't and never will? *Things change. People unmask.*

A broken promise erodes trust but that is not an excuse to build walls around our emotions. Quite the contrary. Having loved, married and divorced is actually a grand opportunity to properly align focus and review the Promise from the most important One.

Deuteronomy 31:6 says that we are not to be afraid or terrified of anyone, anything or any situation that would try to shake our confidence in Him. He sees us from end to beginning to end and is not caught off guard when mess up and our plans fall apart. Yet, He holds true to His promise to never leave nor forsake us. A quick google search of the word promise yields the following as a definition: promise – give good grounds for expecting (a particular occurrence or situation). God's promise is one you can expect to be fulfilled. He is committed to stay with us while we work through the process of becoming what He designed in the first place. No mountain, no valley, no river can keep us separated from God's love and care.

Psalm 139:7-10
Where can I go from Your Spirit?
Where can I flee from Your presence?
If I go up to the heavens, You are there:
If I make my bed in the depths, you are there.

If I rise on the wings of the dawn, if I settle on the far side of the sea, even there Your hand will guide me, your right hand will hold me fast.
We drift away. He won't leave.

Have you ever been sent on assignment to the corner store by your mother for a pack of peanuts and a soda? You ball that money up in your hand and head to the store knowing you betta bring her peanuts and soda fairly quickly. Along the way, you might get a little distracted if you see your friends playing kickball or something. You may even hang out with them for a few minutes but your primary assignment is in the back of your mind. You are tempted to stay and get in the game but your assignment is pressing. Your mother expects you to do what she said in a timely manner. So you run to the store, get the peanuts and soda then run all the way home. *You gotta make up for that time you spent talking to your friends.* That's sorta how it is when God sends His Word to accomplish something in our lives. It does just that. It accomplishes what He sent it to do. The Father has sent a Word of Promise to us that is unlike any promise we might receive from "man". *Because there have been distractions and delays, expect that the Promise will run to you in these days.* His Word is sure. His promises are true. The seas hold their place based on His Word. The stars, sun and moon hang by the Word of our God. *Ain't that something?* A Promise kept builds trust. *Enjoy your peanuts and soda.*

The Provision for Living

God supplies my needs, one day at a time.
Lailah Gifty Akita, Think Great: Be Great

"...our Daily Bread..."
The Provision for Living means getting to know the Provider and living in continued relationship with Him.

If I want you to get to know the "mother" side of me, I will invite you into my space when I am in "mother" mode. Often, our knowledge or perspective of God is so limited until He has to cause us to be in difficult situations so that we can be exposed to another side of Him. Going through divorce caused many different thoughts and emotions. More than I'd ever experienced before. I found that for every positive experience, thought or emotion He is the Source and for every negative experience, thought or emotion, He is the Answer. *I'm lonely.* I AM with you. *I'm weak.* I AM your Strength. *I've lost my way and don't want to live.* I AM the Way, the Truth and the Life.

Before divorce, I'd never really had to extend my faith so far to believe God for basic things like food, utilities or a manicure. In addition to the need for physical things, there was also need for the intangibles like peace, joy and sound mind. Tangible vs intangible is where we get in trouble. It can be difficult to grasp the fact that we really are spirit beings housed inside bodies. This earthly encasement tricks us into believing that temporal things are more important than what's eternal. It goes without saying that while we are in these bodies, we need food, shelter, clothing and other amenities but we cannot let pursuit of earthly things blind us to the fact we are of far greater worth and purpose.

Prior to divorce, I had set morning devotion time when I would spend at least an hour praying and reading scripture. Post divorce was a different story and it became more and more difficult to set aside specific time to study and pray. I will admit, that I began to walk in a bit of condemnation about this. I had, though, began taking my lunch hour to drive certain neighborhoods in our City and pray. I'd go through a drive-thru, grab lunch; drive, eat and pray for an hour then return to my office. One day as I drove, I heard, "this is what I have need of you to do right now– not sit in your room and pray for an hour with your eyes closed." *Okay*

Why are we instructed to pray for our <u>daily</u> bread? Could it be that this is one way God sets it up to spend time with us each day? *Give us THIS day.... We'll be back tomorrow to talk about tomorrow.* Our provision for living is in Him. As we seek His hand, it draws us closer to His face. Not only do we receive the tangible things we need, but we also receive instruction on what to do TODAY.

Perhaps another reason we are instructed to pray for our <u>daily</u> bread is because God doesn't want us to carry anything that is unnecessary. When experiencing divorce, it is so easy to become overwhelmed with financial obligations, in particular. It can be quite a dramatic shift from a two income household to one. You could find yourself shifted from being an at home wife and mother to a single parent head of household situation. Personally, I tried to do too much too fast. That doesn't get you any further ahead. It only adds to the stress level. *Just breathe.* Instead of worrying about what you don't have, learn how to be a good steward of what you do have. *I'm still working on that.* As you pray for the necessities of life, don't forget to feed your spirit and get instruction for daily living. The things we can't see are actually more important than the things that scream for our attention.

Proverbs 30:8-9
Keep falsehood and lies far from me; give me neither poverty nor riches, <u>but give me only my daily</u>

bread. Otherwise, I may have too much and disown You and say, "Who is the Lord?" Or I may steal, and so dishonor the name of my God.

The Postlude
Every new beginning comes from some other beginning's end.
Seneca

Timing is Everything
So! All this time you thought your problem was being single. Now you know that is not the case. Something is still wrong, though. What is it?

Actually, I enjoy being single. I like being able to express my creativity. I love pulling together workshops/concerts and skits, making flyers and posters, going through song selection with the band, long hours of rehearsals with the group and equipment malfunctions. Then after many hours and days of preparation, the hustle and bustle of the concert day is quite exhilarating especially when everything is "on". The group sings outta the "city of their soul" and the band is unleashed. After all has been said, done and "all hearts and minds are clear", I can't stand going home……. alone. *Hmmm*

Could the real problem be that YOU just don't like being alone? Often times single people tend to get very involved with various ministries, activities and committees to stay occupied – to keep from being alone. "No man is an island" is a well-known, often used and very true saying. We were not made to be isolated from other people. God, in His infinite wisdom, made us relational/social beings.

Two are better than one, because they have a good reward for their labor. For if they fall, one will lift up his companion. Ecclesiastes 4:9

And they continued steadfastly in the apostles' doctrine and fellowship in the breaking of bread and in prayers. Now all who believed were together and had all things common. Acts 2:42,44

The desire for companionship is as natural as breathing. I am not, however, convinced that marriage will quench that desire. I know you remember Leah (Genesis 29). She was married with children but still without the companionship of her husband. She had sex, as evidenced by the birthing of her children, but never really connected with Jacob. Why?

Jacob, through no real fault of his own, never saw Leah until after their marriage was consummated. Leah entered the marital relationship in darkness, under a cloak of deception. *Read the scripture.* No real fault of hers, either. *That's just how it was done.* Leading the bride into the bedchamber of the groom in secrecy and darkness was a custom of that time. I contend that it is a custom of our time, as well. We don't always tell or portray the truth about ourselves to our intended mate. Sometimes we go into a relationship determined that we are going to "get" him or her no matter the cost. We lie, cheat and steal all to get someone that, in a few years - - sometimes months or days we are ready to throw back! *I just want what I want and don't care how I get it.* Sometimes we are the deceiver. Other times we are the deceived. I realize Jacob couldn't see Leach through the darkness and deception but I've wondered if a little flag was raised with him at any time. We can want what we want sooo bad until we ignore the flags and warning signs about what's ahead.

What's ahead - - hmmm. Although Jacob was hung up on what looked good physically, (Genesis 29:30) his ultimate blessing and that of all mankind, came through the ugly woman (Genesis 29:35, Matthew 1:1-6, Luke 3:31-34, Revelation 5:5). During all the time that Leah was unloved, essentially alone and rejected, no one knew what was going on deep inside of her. I never see in the scriptures where anyone offered her a word of encouragement or advice. Not even Leah knew the significance of what was in her but when she mustered up enough strength to push out a real praise (Judah), she set things in motion for the greatest miracle of all times. Was not the Messiah birth through the line of

Judah? Leah was not the best looking or the best loved but there was something IN her that all of us need. A praise. *What am I hearing?* ***"Some awesome promises will be birth out of your ugly stuff".*** I know you're hurting and sad now and no one seems to understand or be able to offer any real help. But what if the promise that's inside you is just too valuable to expose right now? This just is not the time. It's there. It's special. Its magnificent. Just….not….*now.* When!?

One of my all-time favorite songs is The Rose by Bette Midler. The last verse says: *"When the night has been too lonely and the road has been too long. And you think that love is only for the lucky and the strong. Just remember in the winter far beneath the bitter snow, lies the seed that with the sun's love, in the spring becomes the rose."*

At the onset of my season of singleness, I had no idea that it would be such a loooong winter. *Have you ever been so cold until you couldn't feel your fingers or toes? Try that for YEARS. Numb.* Think about this, though. What would it be like to have summer all year? Nature would not have the opportunity to reset herself and rejuvenate the earth. There would be no cold weather to kill mosquitoes and bugs. No balance. Winter is necessary. *To everything there is a season, and a time to every purpose under the heaven.*

Everything about your past is not going to make sense. The naked truth is this. You may never know why the relationship(s) didn't work, why **he** "messed with" you when you were just a child, why **she** gave you away or why **they** don't support you; but while you're reading this book, notice the rise and fall of your chest as you breathe. Be encouraged. It's not over. It's about TIME. Go on. Rejoice in your season of singleness and know "…He hath made everything beautiful in…His…time…" (Ecclesiastes 3:11a)

The Prologue
The fat lady ain't even tuned up yet.
Cynthia Mitchell

#myturningpoint

Moment of transparency: I began this particular writing in 2006. The manuscript sat in a pile of stuff for well over ten years. I never felt the "release" to publish it until now. As I reviewed the work to complete it, I realized I had the last section labeled "Postlude" but at the top of the very next page, I'd typed "Prologue". Hmm. That's not proper.

Postlude – a <u>concluding</u> piece of music, especially an organ piece played at the end of a religious service; a written or spoken epilogue, an afterword.

Prologue – a <u>separate introductory</u> section of a literary or musical work; <u>an event or action that leads to another event or situation</u>.

So, after what I originally thought to be the end, there is a beginning.

In 2014, I married who I believed was my knight in shining armor. *Turned out to be a jackass in aluminum foil. Let's talk about this.* For the sake of civility from this point forward, we will call him MrGoodFella. *And that is not a typo. I meant to run it all together…just…like…that.*

It would be too much to recount all of the inconsistencies that I really began to notice on the day of the wedding. I'll just sum it up like this: *I did not live a double life before I met you and I will not start now, Sir.* So, there I was, at the point of living what should have been the realization of my lifelong dream – life, ministry and businesses with my husband but I was actually fast approaching a very significant turning point in my life.

In hindsight, I recognize that I talked too much at the beginning of the relationship. I was quite open about my heart's desires and he played the part as long as he could. *One thing about it, what's IN you will eventually come out.* After MrGoodFella, I unplugged for about two years – no church – no music, not even on the radio – no engagements or assignments. Just work, home and sleep. I needed as much silence as possible. Then, as I began to shake it off, I spent many days and nights questioning everything. I said, "God, SOMEbody is lyin'!" Initially, I questioned everything about ME. There was no need to question anything more regarding MrGoodFella. *That ship had sailed and sank.* As I questioned myself, I finally admitted that my primary reason for marrying *THAT one* at that particular time was because I was concerned about my natural and ministry children more than myself. Even though my children were grown, I still wanted them to have a "dad" to develop relationship with - someone who could help them navigate young adulthood. Since the two of us had already been through so much, I thought we would be able to stop the cycle in both our bloodlines and show our children how to steer clear of divorce. My group was ministering at an uncommon level at the time and I didn't want to fall off the "sexual abstinence wagon" again, derail the ministry and negatively impact the young lives attached to it. *Reminder to Self: God doesn't need my help.*

When I got to the point of wanting to question God, I realized that I couldn't even go there. I'd seen Him bring me through so many things, so many times. Little things, big things – things I'd only prayed about and never breathed a word to anyone.

I've seen Him do it! Did I tell you about the time in 2000, when I found myself in dire need of a tire for my Ford Explorer? I pulled into the tire dealership hoping they could patch one tire, in particular, and let me roll on a little while longer. I was sitting in the waiting area when the store manager came over to me and said, "Ma'am, all of your tires are bad and

I especially can't let you drive outta here on the one tire that is beyond repair." He went on to say, "BUT (*THIS is the part where I start shouting EV'RY time.*) it just so happens there is a recall on the brand of tires that's on your vehicle. We JUST got the notice. It hasn't even gone public yet. I can go on and replace all of your tires, including your spare, at no charge to you". *Yeah! That huge tire recall back in 2000 was all about me. Ha.* In the very second that I needed reassurance about who and Whose I am, that tire situation came to mind. So, God had not lied. *He was saying, "Remember My track record with you. I got you".* There was still another layer to this situation – something God needed me to taste.

My experiences with MrGoodFella confirmed three Truths that I will forever cling to with every fiber of my being.

#1: It's not that God won't lie. He can't lie and when you diligently seek Him, He avails Himself to you. He won't leave you hangin'.

#2: The things we go through in life, particularly the dark things, are ordained to give us deeper revelation of God's Word and His plans. Just as with Hosea, there will be times when we have to just hold our heads up and live through things that cause us to look foolish. *#gazingstock Hebrews 10:33* We will not be able to deliver what He requires if we have not gone through the process. We must TASTE that thang because in the very second that we are required to execute, we must do so without doubt or wavering.

#3: I believe that MrGoodFella basically embodied a type and shadow of what is going on with "the church" in this hour. Why do I say that? I'm glad you asked.

"The Church" has fluffed and puffed all we can. We've put on perfume but have not bathed. This church culture of "suddenly" and "pack your bags, you're going to the nations" - with all of the theatrics and emotionalism has produced shallow, lazy, rude, immature and impotent people. We lack the power, strength and vigor to perform………..in righteousness. We're chasing a prophecy while still bound, broken and bleeding. There is no condemnation in being bound, broken and bleeding. *Just don't stay there too long.* Each of us has our own set of assigned demons to deal with and it is not easy. Too often, instead of effectively dealing with those things, we dress them up in cute little outfits and make them a part of our entourage. NOW (in this hour), individually and collectively, we must face the things that have caused impotence and affected our performance in the Kingdom. SOME things we should have killed a long time ago. They will not be easily moved now. Other things will challenge us at the very core of our belief.

The church culture has layered lie upon lie – deceit on top of deceit. But it is not about lies/liars being exposed. That is low level operation. In this hour, Truth is being revealed. It is not okay to put on ya li'l collar and ministry outfit, go preach the paint off walls somewhere then go home and talk to/treat your spouse/family any ole kinda way. It's not okay to be a Prophet in public but indulge in perversion in private. We will *noT* continue to hold up the prayer line every Sunday, foolin' with you when all you really need to do is keep your legs closed. Who said that being in fulltime ministry means that you just don't work and cause unnecessary financial hardship on your spouse/family? *That's not how any of this works.* Lazy. Rude. Immature. Impotent. Who said that this generation is wrong to rebuff a man made doctrine that takes focus off God and seeks to manipulate and control people? *Who said?!* There has to come a turning point in all of this. We gotta get out of this cycle of madness. *Some of you may be a little salty about the "fulltime ministry/just don't work" statement. I do believe that some people are called full time to the work of the ministry. I also know there are false prophets and lazy people among us operating like scam artists, looking for a free ride. If you let'em ride they gone try to drive - - drive you straight to the poor house with a stop at the crazy house on the way. We just tryna slay some demons here.*

Why am I writing about this? Because I know there are too many people operating in the church while losing at life. Many are trying to live up to an image while bound, broken, bleeding, mistreated, used and abused. I did that for many years without even realizing what, exactly, I was doing– trying to live up to "church" expectations. *#stopit* I want you to be encouraged and know that there is a bend in the road just ahead. I don't care how long you have been in that place. It really doesn't matter how many times you've made a mess of things. This is your reset button. The old things are passed away. THIS is the introductory section to an entirely new place for you.

…consider God's Plan for YOU – not necessarily marriage. Get the vision of your expected end.

...examine, closely, the Pain you've experienced as a result of relationship(s). It didn't kill you. Learn from it. Keep moving forward.

...embrace the Process of healing and don't be afraid to reinvent yourself, if necessary.

...confront the root Problem to avoid repetitive cycles of internal conflict. Research your family history and your personal intimate history.

...hold on to the Promise of The Father. Once you settle with who and Whose you are, every other thing falls into place.

...steward the Provision well. All you need to survive and thrive is already in you.

At the end of the day, I don't hold anything against MrGoodFella. *We have to stop expecting people to give us what they don't have.* Perhaps, I am simply a hopeless romantic. There IS a "happily ever after." I refuse to believe that chivalry is dead. I still believe that it is possible to have a genuine, loving, Kingdom marriage. I also know that the best relationships take work. All of which must begin internally.

So, I'm single…..again. Now what? I will forgive myself and others. I will be better, never bitter. I will live and in this, my Prologue of life, I will embrace my turning point.

In three words, I can sum up everything I've learned about life: "It goes on".
Robert Frost

Made in the USA
Columbia, SC
14 December 2024